Okay, We Grew Old Together...
NOW WHAT?

Questions for celebrating your best moments, memories and milestones while considering what the heck you want to do next!

A COUPLE'S JOURNAL

by

Annette Bridges

© 2020 Annette Bridges

www.annettebridges.com

Published by Ranch House Press

All rights reserved. Except as permitted under the U.S. Copyright Act of 1976, no part of this publication may be reproduced, distributed, or transmitted in any form or by any means, or stored in a database or retrieval system, without prior written permission of the author.

Doodle Art by Annette Bridges

Layout and Cover Design by Callie Revell
www.callierevell.com

Printed in the United States of America

ISBN 978-1-946371-46-1

INTRODUCTION

This journal has been created for old married folks, long-timers and long-termers. In other words, it's a journal for those couples in a long-lasting marriage or partnership of twenty, thirty, forty or more years.

When I tell people we've been married for thirty-nine years, I get a reaction of shock and awe. I'm not sure if they are amazed by the number (as in, "that's a long time"), or maybe they are impressed that we have been together so long and still in love with each other.

In celebration of our anniversary this year, I was inspired to create this journal because frankly, the questions you'll find here are ones I've been gathering for a while and are ones that I want us to answer together.

We are both in our seventh decade, and the truth is, we've been stuck in idle lately wondering about what to do next in our lives. Dreaming new dreams are not as easy to do as they once were. As we muddle our way through dreads and fears of seniorhood, it seems like it may be useful and helpful to reminisce on our most precious memories and happiest of times as we look for ways to have many more during the rest of our life together. I'm also thinking that pondering sweet moments may make considering some of the harder questions easier.

I plan to remind myself there is no one right or wrong way to answer these questions since I'm pretty sure my partner and I will not answer in the same way. Being married to a man who often expresses himself in few words, my desire is to understand and value his feelings, fears and longings as much as I want him to do the same for mine. My hope is that this journal provides us a tool to do just that. And I hope you and your partner find it beneficial as well regardless of how long you've been together!

Annette Bridges

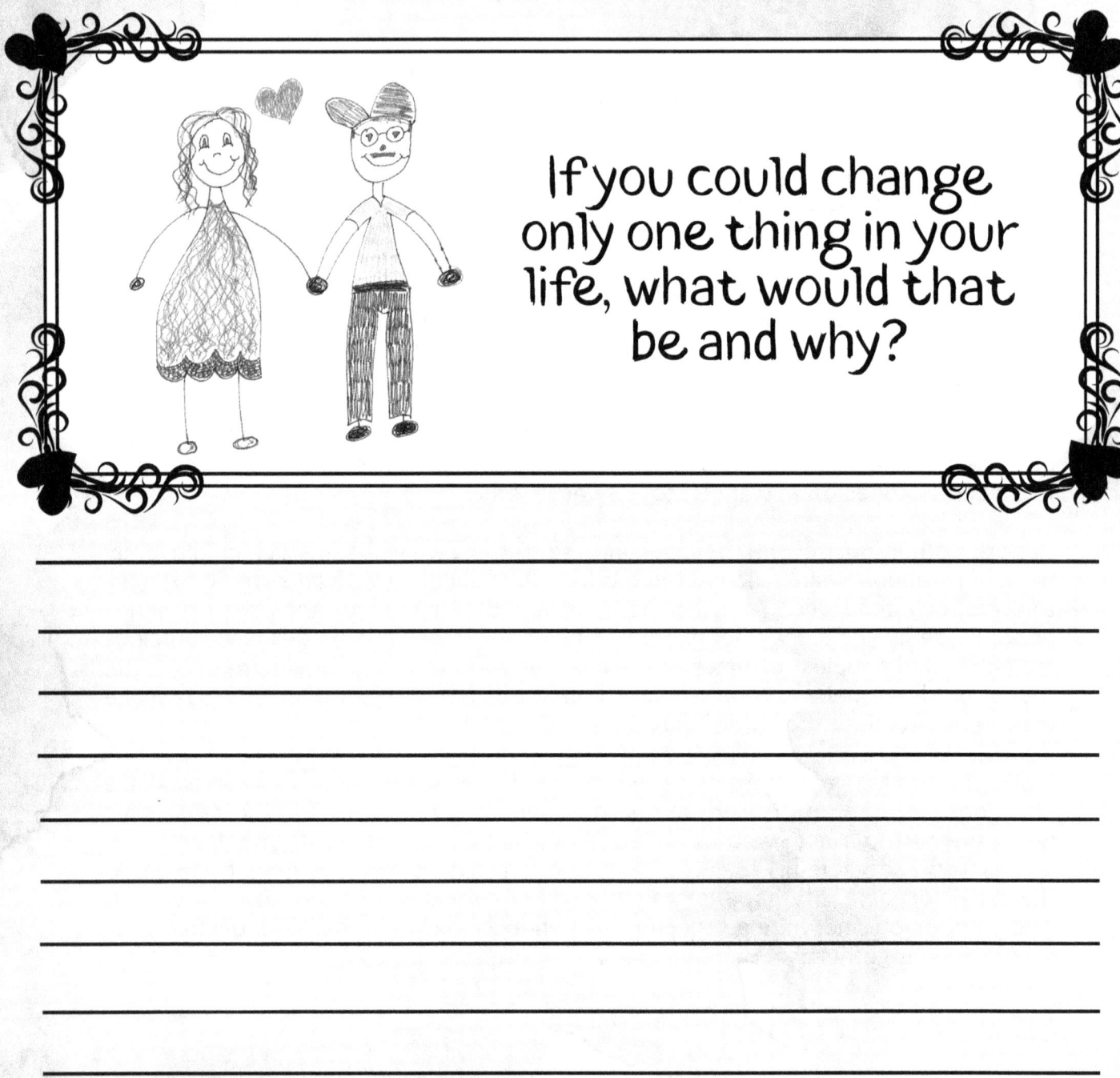

If you could change only one thing in your life, what would that be and why?

In a regular day, what do you find yourself thinking about the most?

If you could write a song about your life, what type of music would you use?

What things in your life bring you the greatest pleasure?

What do you feel is your greatest accomplishment in your life?

In what settings are you the happiest/most eager/most comfortable?

_____
_____
_____
_____
_____
_____
_____
_____

What things do you look forward to each day?

If you had three wishes that would come true, what would they be?

What other things would you want to change now, and why?

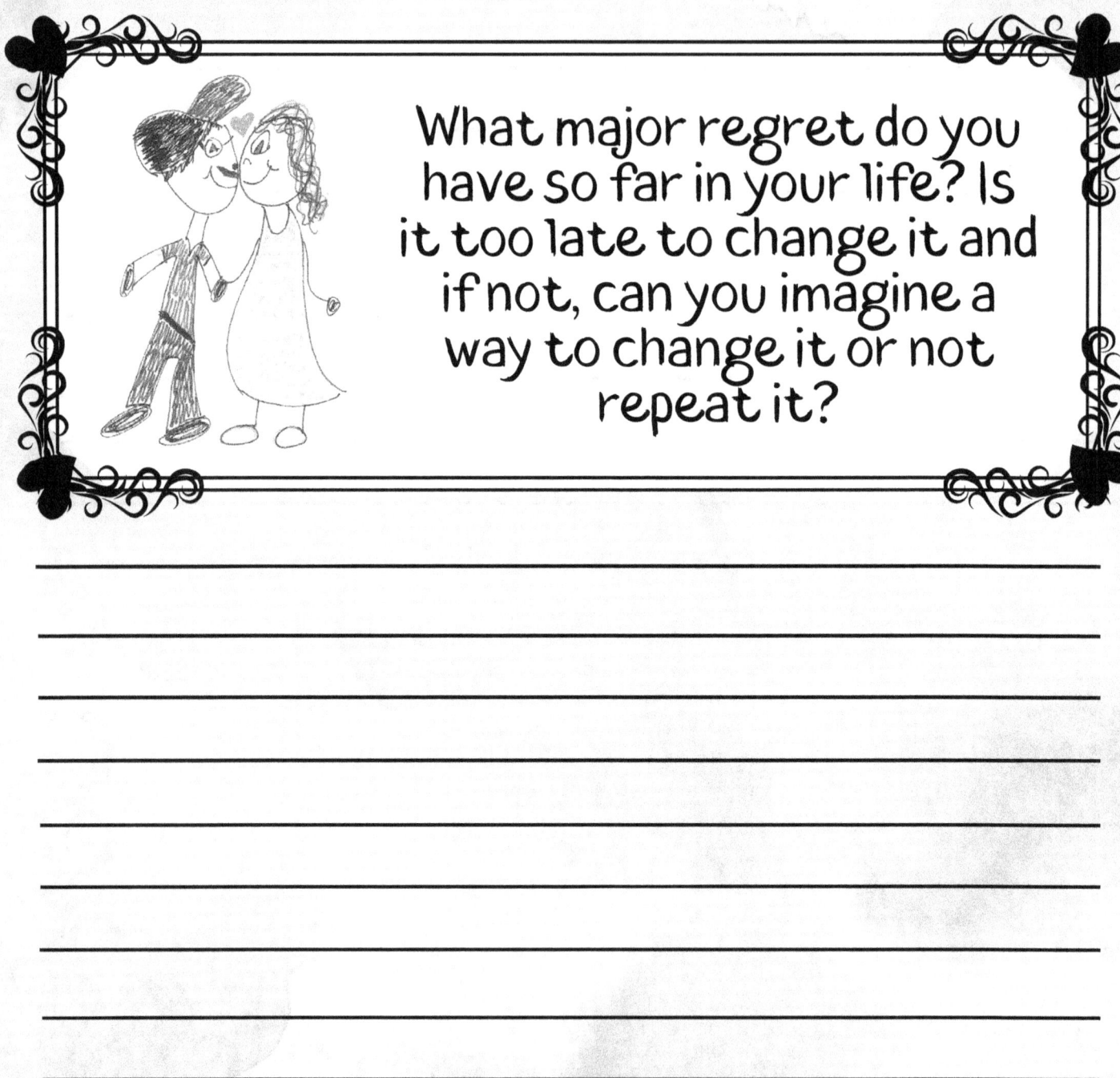

What major regret do you have so far in your life? Is it too late to change it and if not, can you imagine a way to change it or not repeat it?

What would be your ideal romantic date?

What would you like to do outdoors that you have not done before?

Name 3 things that most excite your imagination when you imagine doing them.

What are your favorite things to spend money on?

Describe your ideal weekend.

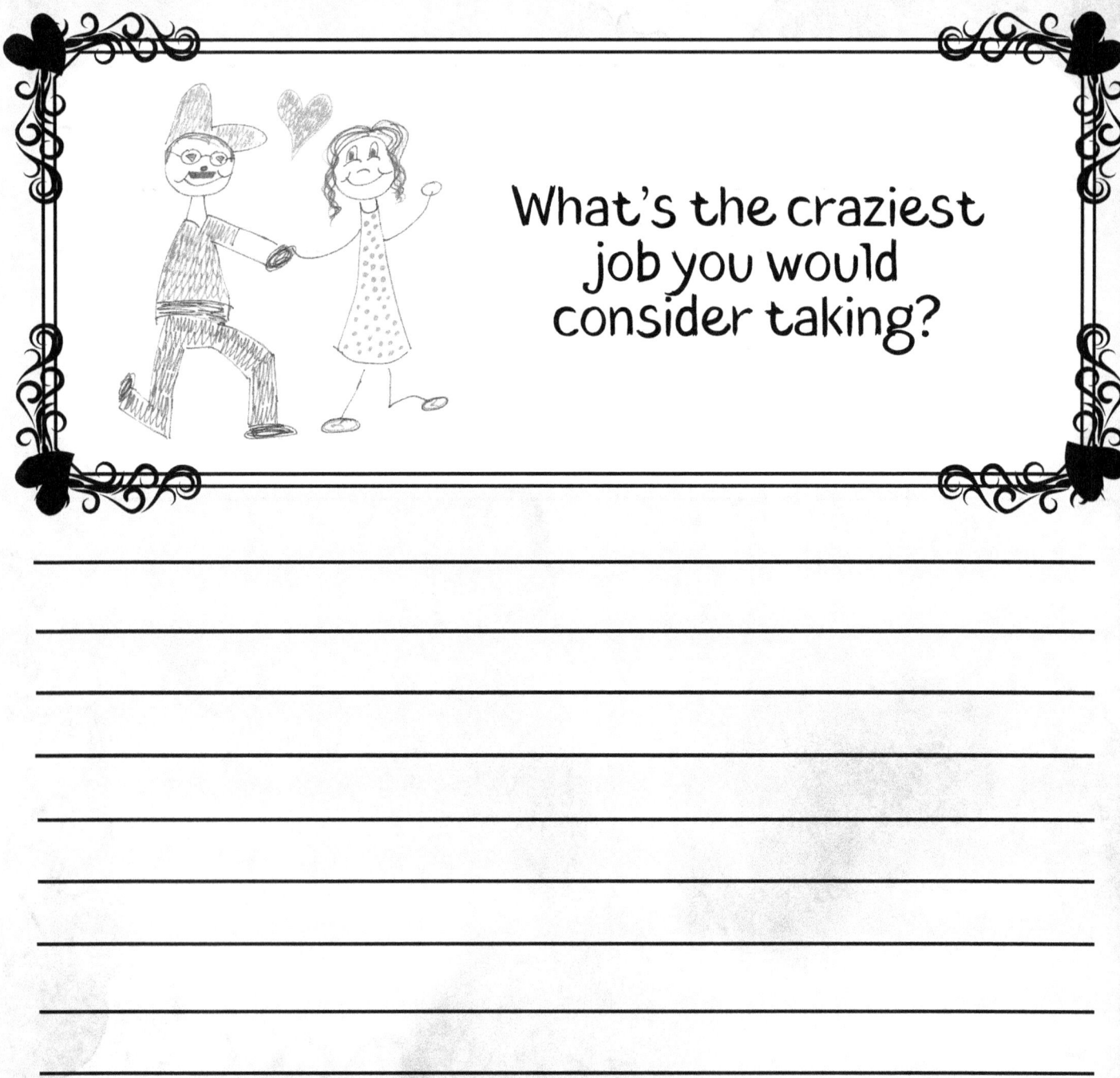

What's the craziest job you would consider taking?

If you had to spend 1 million dollars in one day, what would you buy?

What is the most expensive thing you have ever bought?

What's the most impulsive thing you've ever done?

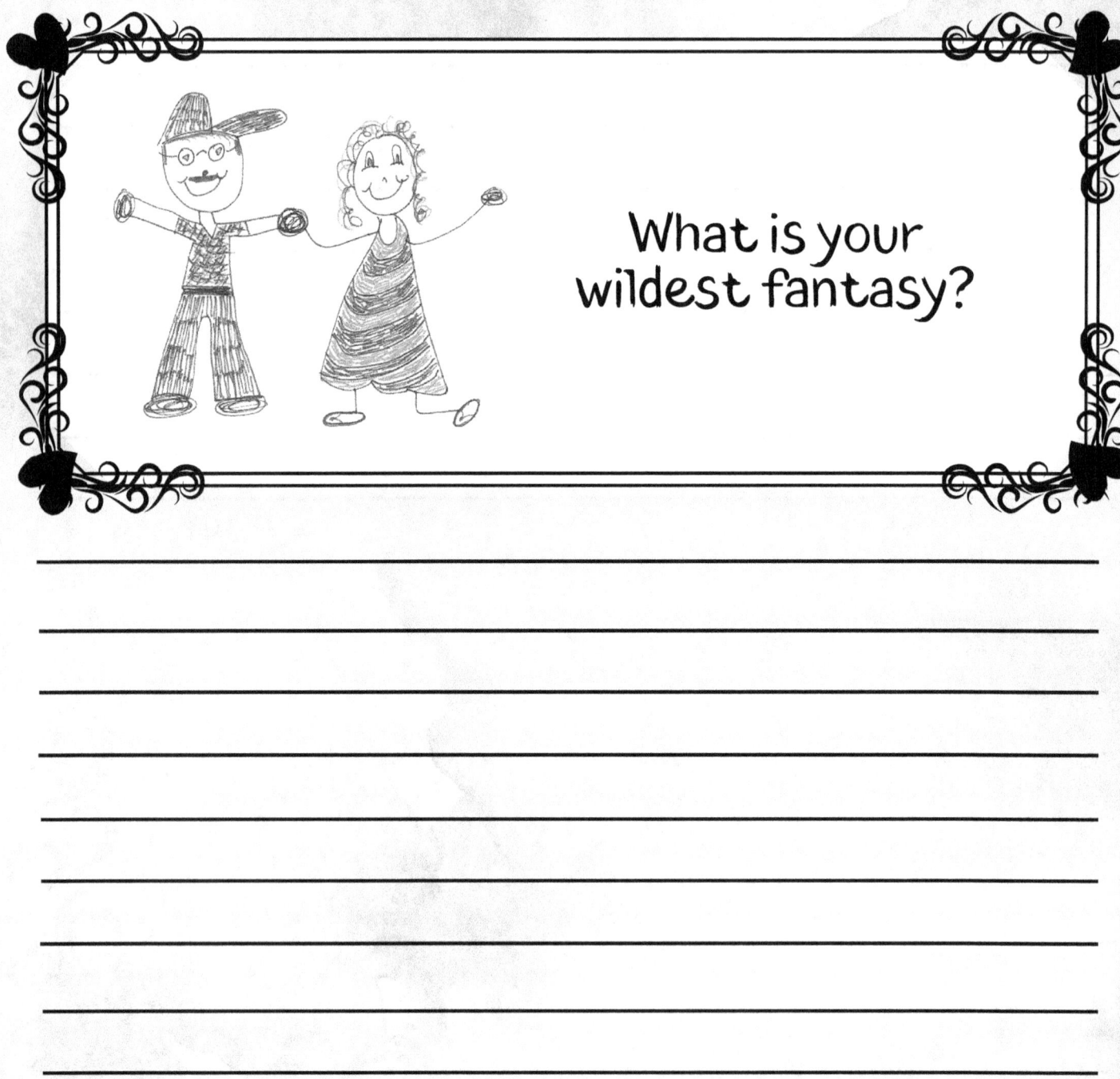

What is your wildest fantasy?

What do you think makes your partner smile?

What's the most romantic thing your partner has ever done for you?

What's your favorite trait of your partner?

What would be your ideal romantic date?

What's one thing about your relationship with your mate that makes you the happiest?

Which song comes to your mind and heart that reminds you of your mate?

What do you find yourself insecure about?

What scares you the most?

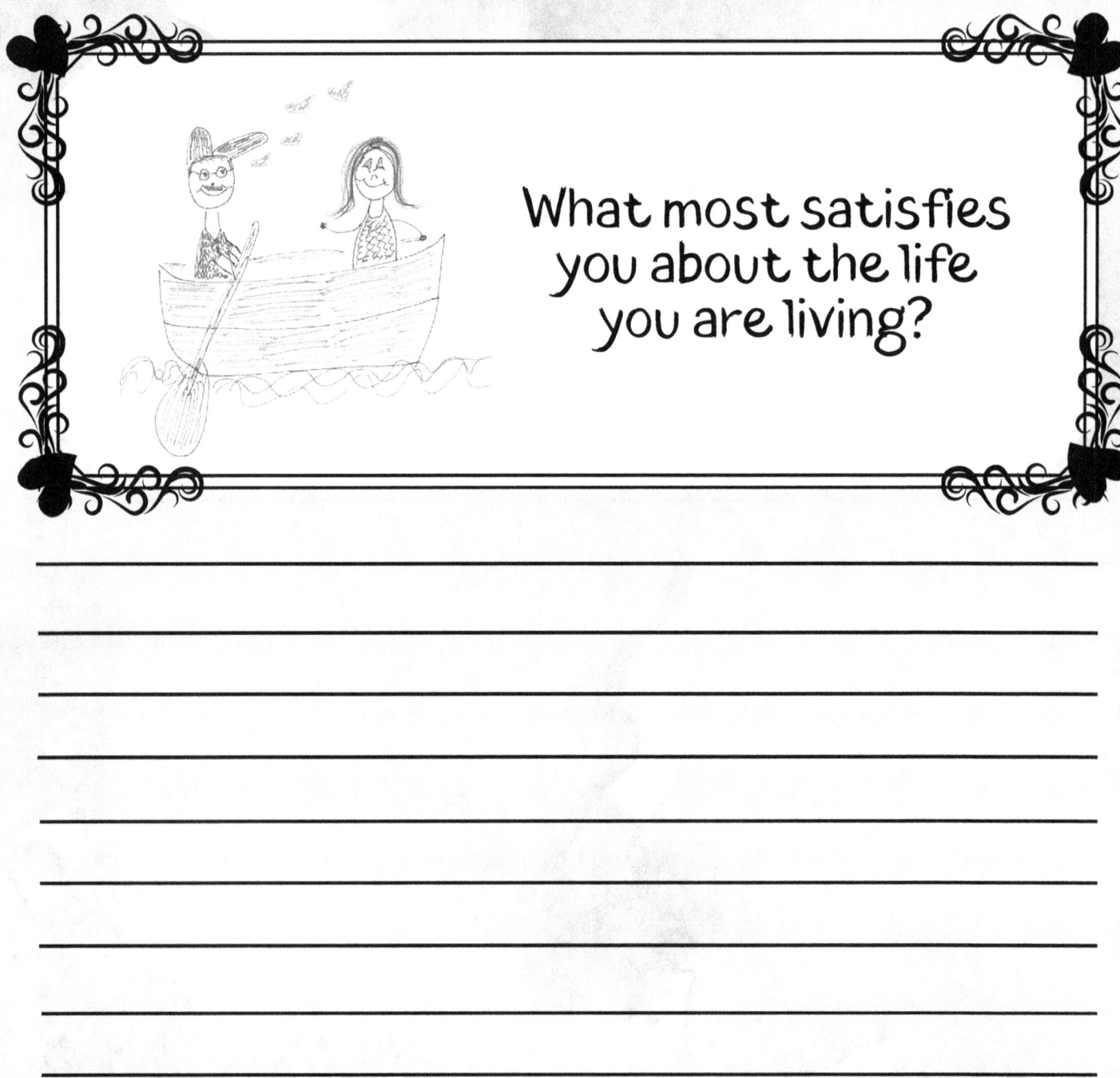

What most satisfies you about the life you are living?

What was the very first thing you thought about your partner when you met?

What's the main thing you need from your partner?

What is missing from your marriage right now, and how do you think you both could fix what's missing?

Describe a happy and fun day that you'll never forget.

What are you the most excited about for your future?

What are three of your biggest needs, and how could your partner help you fulfill them?

What is the best part of being together with your spouse?

Name three things that you and your partner appear to have in common.

For what in your life do you feel most grateful?

What is something you've dreamed of doing for a long time but haven't?

What do you value most in your relationship?

Describe something you like about your partner.

What's something you want you and your partner to do in the next year that you've never done before?

What's a favorite memory you've shared together?

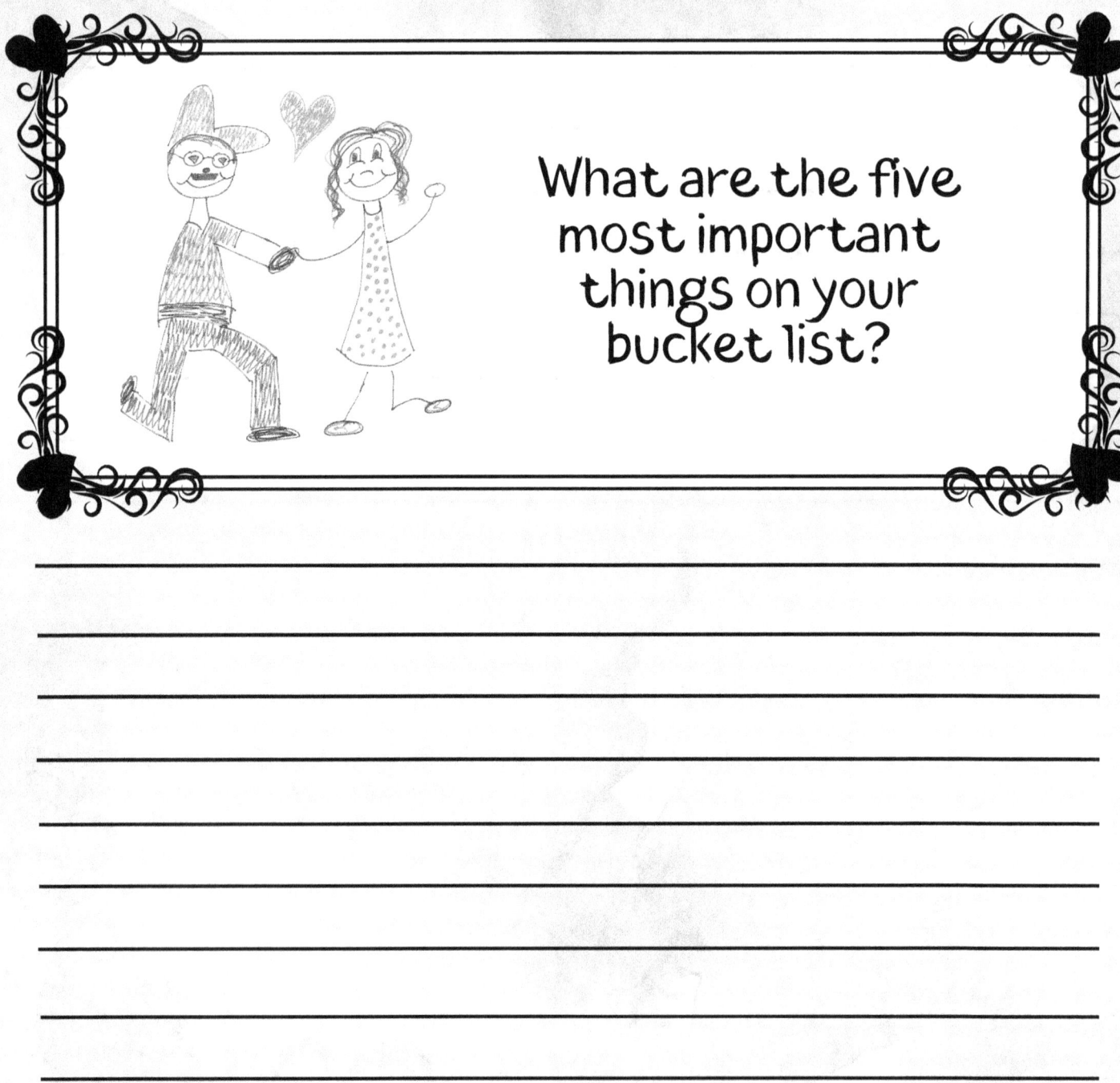

What are the five most important things on your bucket list?

What's something your partner did for you that you're grateful for?

What do you want your legacy to be?

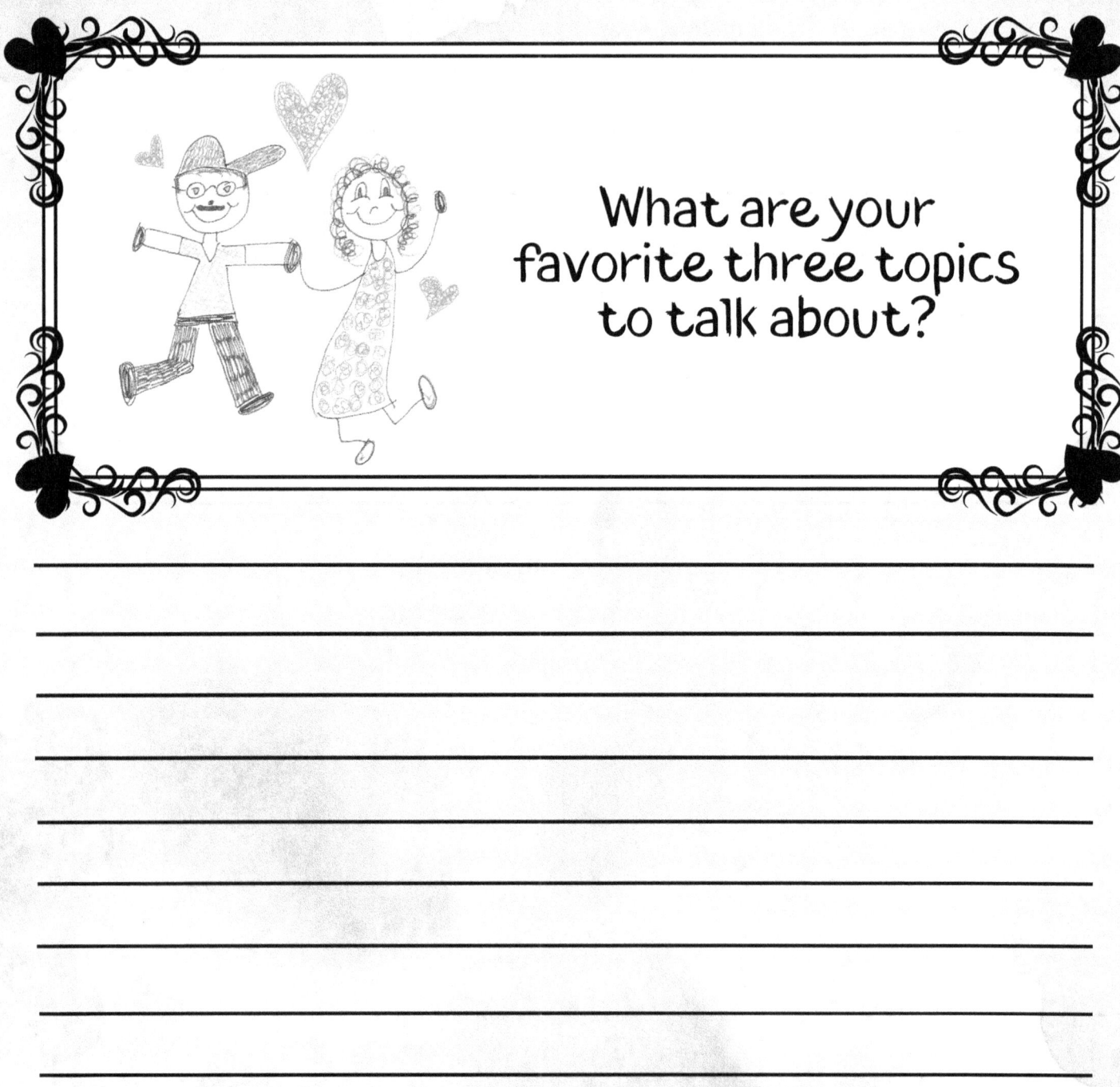

What are your favorite three topics to talk about?

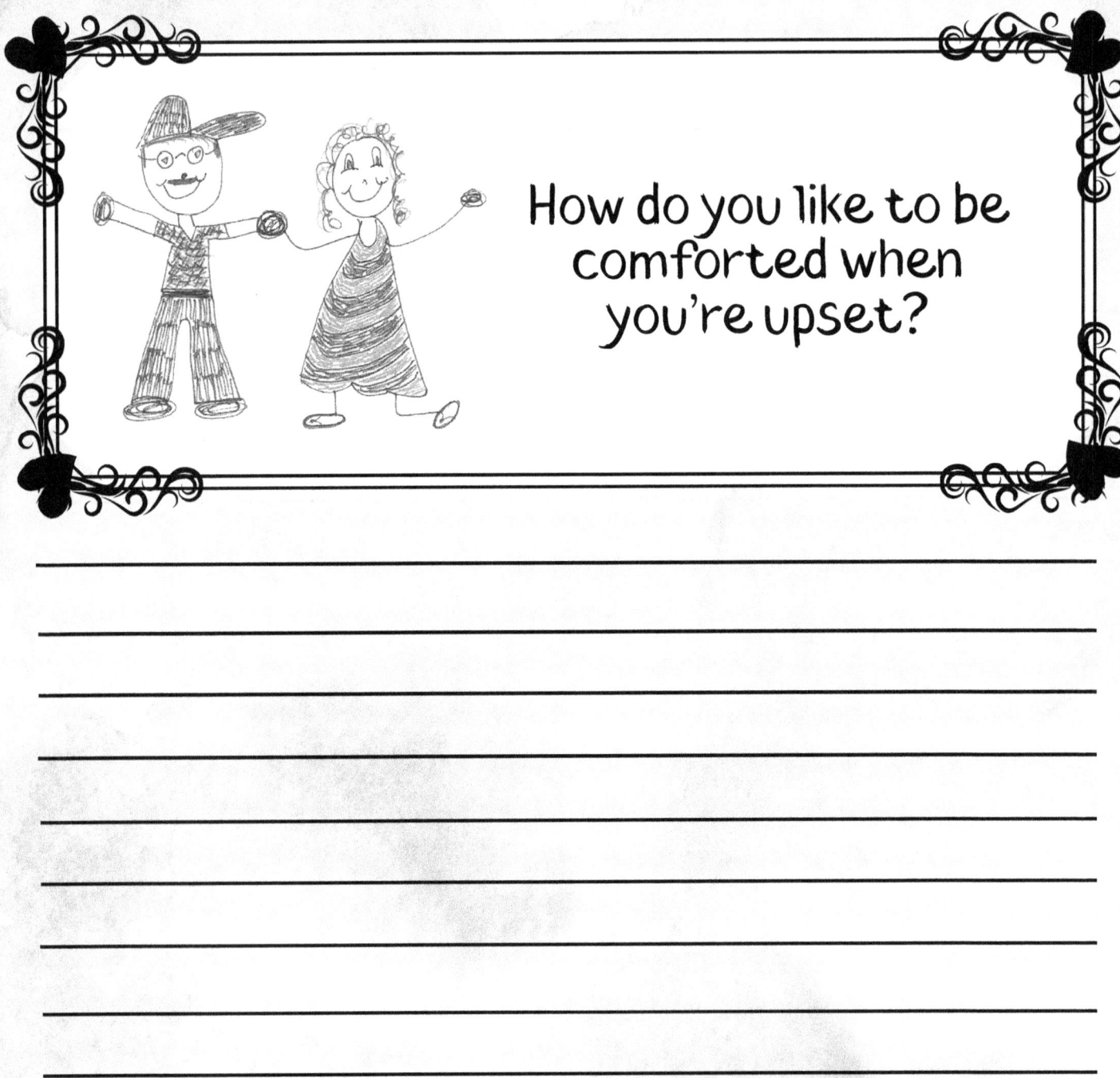

How do you like to be comforted when you're upset?

In ten years, how would you like to describe your life?

Write your own questions you want you and your partner to answer!

About the Author & Artist
ANNETTE BRIDGES

Annette Bridges is a cattle rancher, magazine columnist and Ranch House Gift Shop owner. She is an author and the founder of Ranch House Press, a publisher of books, journals and more than empower, encourage and entertain. She has published nonfiction books, coloring books, journals and even a cookbook for children.

Before writing books, this former public and homeschool educator spent a decade writing instructive and lighthearted columns for Texas newspapers, magazines and websites. Today, Annette writes a monthly lifestyle column titled "When a city girl goes country" featured in *North Texas Farm and Ranch Magazine.*

In Annette's Ranch House Gift Shop on Etsy, you'll find all of her books and other print products along with many fun specialty items including jewelry and t-shirts.

For thirty-nine years, Annette has lived on a north Texas cattle ranch with her husband, John. She can drive a tractor and do other ranch chores, but only if she's wearing a fresh coat of lipstick and it's not her pedicure day!

You can learn more about Annette and read her archived magazine columns at her website: **www.annettebridges.com**. And if you love cows or need some inspiration and giggles, be sure to follow her Texas author page on Facebook at **www.facebook.com/TexasAuthorAnnetteBridges**.

Also By Annette...

Color-N-Doodle Your World
An inspiring collection of coloring pages with your own space to doodle and create.

My Furry Friend
A keepsake journal.

A Dachshund Tale
Lessons learned from my dog.

Color Your World Journal Series
18 themed journals.

Jot Journals
18 themed pocket-sized journals.

Oh, How the Years Fly By!
A whimsical adult coloring book.

Oh, How the Years Fly By!
A whimsical inspirational quote book.

The Gospel According to Mamma
One mother's philosophy on love, God, money, aging, decisions, change, and much more.

Be Queen of Your Life
A savvy mom helps daughters command and rule their lives.

Have Lipstick, Will Travel
How to reimagine your life, purpose, and hair color.

Lady and Bella: Totally Different, Totally Friends
A coloring storybook for children.

Lady and Bella: Totally Friends Journal
Especially for children.

Lady and Bella's Alphabet Kitchen
A to Z recipes for kid cooks.

www.ingramcontent.com/pod-product-compliance
Lightning Source LLC
Chambersburg PA
CBHW081750100526
44592CB00015B/2361